doggie days

♥

love guide

WEST HIGHLAND TERRIER

Other Doggie Days Products:
Wall Calendars

Beagle	West Highland	Chocolate Lab
Dachshund	Border Collie	Dalmatian
German Shepherd	Boston Terrier	Poodle
Golden Retriever	Boxer	Pug
Jack Russell Terrier	Bulldog	Siberian Husky
Labrador Retriever	Bull Terrier	Welsh Corgi
Rottweiler	Chihuahua	Cocker Spaniel

Dated Engagement Calendars

Doggie Days Engagement Calendars

Books

Doggie Days Love Guide Jack Russell	*Doggie Days Love Guide* West Highland
Doggie Days Love Guide Poodle	*Doggie Days Love Guide* Golden Retriever
Doggie Days Love Guide Pug	*Doggie Days Love Guide* Beagle
Doggie Days Love Guide Chihuahua	*Doggie Days Love Guide* Labrador Retriever
Doggie Days Love Guide Welsh Corgi	*Doggie Days Love Guide* German Shepherd

Design and Photography © Leslie Evans Design Associates, Inc.
Design and Art Direction by Leslie Evans
Photographs by Shoshannah White for Leslie Evans Design Associates, Inc.
Text written by and © 2004 Ronnie Sellers

Westies courtesy of:
Breemoor Westies, Rockland, Me., breemoor@earthlink.net

Published by Ronnie Sellers Productions, Inc.
81 West Commercial Street, Portland, Maine 04101
www.makefun.com, E-mail: rsp@rsvp.com
ISBN: 1-56906-552-7
Printed in China

10 9 8 7 6 5 4 3 2 1

CONTENTS

1

CHAPTER 1
What I Look for When I'm Looking for Love

2

CHAPTER 2
To Know Me Is to Love Me

3

CHAPTER 3
Love Me Forever

4

CHAPTER 4
Love Journal

Introduction

♥

I'm not just any dog, I'm a

West Highland Terrier.
I'm a Hug Hound!

I also have excellent instincts.

I can sniff out Westie lovers

from miles away. This book tells you

everything you need to know to

win my love for life.

CHAPTER 1
What I Look for When I'm Looking for Love

I have a very upbeat personality. I want someone who is fun, someone who will make me smile.

When **interviewing** prospective owners, question #1 is always,

"How big is your yard?"

I need room to play. Question #2 is,

"How big is your bed?"

I need room to sleep. Question #3 is,

"How big is your heart?"

I need **room** for ME.

I'm extremely **agile**, and I **love** to show off **my tricks**.

But I don't **work** for **free**.

If I dance for you, I expect to be rewarded with a **treat**.

I have tons of energy, so I need lots of exercise, and two walks a day. If you're a couch potato, get yourself a hamster.

I might look like a dog, but I think of myself as a person trapped in a dog's body. I want to be treated like a member of the family.

I'm very social, and I love being with people.

I hate workaholics!

If you think you can leave me home alone for more than eight hours, forgetaboutit!

I'm a small dog, but I need a whole lotta love! Ten hugs a day, minimum! And guess what, you can take me with you! I'm the original Porta-Pooch.

I like to get up close and personal, so you better not have a problem with dog breath. Will you mind if I give you a big wet one every once in a while?

CHAPTER 2
To Know Me Is to Love Me

My coat is pure white,

but my heart is true blue.

Treat me with kindness and

I will always look up to you.

I'm the **type of dog** that likes to **keep on top** of things around the house. If any **strangers** come around, **believe me,** I'll make some NOISE!

As dogs go, I'm pretty smart.

Take me to doggie school, and

I'll make an excellent student.

But don't be fooled by my

serious side.

When I'm not in school,

I can be a real party animal.

My philosophy is:

Play first, ask questions later.

I have one of the best noses in the business, so don't bother trying to hide food from me.

And guess what?

When it comes to biscuits, I Ain't Too Proud to Beg!

The **only thing** that's harder to **keep clean** than a white carpet is a **white dog.** I'll need a **bath and shampoo** at least once a month, sometimes more. And a good **brushing** every few days will **keep** my coat **nice and shiny.**

I dig digging, do you dig? I was bred to burrow. If I live with you, your back yard is going to be one of the holiest places in the neighborhood.

I play **hard,** and I burn

lots of energy.

When it's time to **eat**

I can really put away

some chow. I need

two meals: one in the

morning and one at **night.**

I'm a dog.

Sometimes I pass

a little gas.

Get over it!

CHAPTER 3
Love Me Forever

Promise to care for me.

Immunization Record

AGE	Date Given	Rabies	Distemper	Hepatitis	Parvovirus	Coronavirus	Parainfluenza	Kennel Cough	Lyme Disease	
WKS										
WKS										
WKS										
WKS										
WKS										
1 YEAR										
2 YEAR										
3 YEAR										
4 YEAR										
5 YEAR										
6 YEAR										
7 YEAR										
8 YEAR										
9 YEAR										
10 YEAR										
11 YEAR										
12 YEAR										
13 YEAR										
14 YEAR										
15 YEAR										

In sickness and in health.

Signs that I'm sick
and should see the veterinarian

- I'm not as spunky as usual and I withdraw.

- I stop eating and/or decrease the amount of water I drink.

- I have heavy discharge from my eyes or nose.

- I cough excessively or pant without apparent reason.

- I behave in ways that are unusual.

- I show signs of being in pain, such as limping, yelping, or reacting to being touched in certain places.

- I have trouble urinating or eliminating.

- I have diarrhea or vomiting that persists for more than 24-48 hours.

- I shake my head, scratch, or lick myself excessively.

Promise to **shelter** me

and **protect** me, and **keep**

me from losing my way.

Don't lose your love puppy

- When outside, always keep your dog on a leash.

- Create a fenced play area for your dog if possible.

- Register your dog with your local municipality and make sure to fasten the tag to its collar securely.

- Purchase a separate tag engraved with the dog's name and your name, address, and phone number, as well as any important information (i.e. "Not good with kids," or "I am diabetic").

- Tattoo an I.D. number or your name and phone number on the dog's inner thigh

- Have a microchip implanted. Ask your veterinarian for details.

Promise to be **patient** and kind. I want **more than** anything else to **please** you, but I'm not perfect.

House training

- Begin with paper training. Confine your dog within a space with several layers of paper on the floor.

- Put a small amount of its urine on the paper.

- Once the dog has eliminated on the paper, remove the top layers. The dog's scent will remain.

- Praise the dog when it goes on the paper, but do not punish it when it doesn't. Simply clean up after it with an enzyme cleaner (NOT ammonia) and try again later.

- Place the dog on the paper often until it learns to go there on its own when it needs to eliminate.

- Take your dog outside first thing in the morning, before you go to bed, and at regular intervals in between.

- Begin by taking it to the same spot each time and using the same command such as "go pee."

- Once your dog learns to eliminate outside, begin varying the places that you take it to for that purpose (so it won't become too attached to the original spot).

Help me **learn** to do all the things that **good dogs do.**

Obedience training

- *Begin as early as possible:* by the time a puppy is 8 to 10 weeks old, it is capable of learning basic commands such as "sit," "down," and "come."
- *Be consistent:* use the same verbal commands every time to avoid confusion, and make sure that you enforce the same rules from day to day.
- *Use positive reinforcement:* like people, dogs respond better to positive reinforcement than they do reprimands. Use food treats to reward proper responses.
- *Choose the best time and place to train your dog:* if you are using treats to reinforce behavior, schedule your sessions before mealtime. Find a quiet place without distractions.
- *Be assertive and firm:* dogs are pack animals, and must understand that you are "the leader of the pack."
- *Enroll in formal obedience training classes:* every dog, even an older dog, will benefit from obedience training classes that are conducted by trained professionals. Most obedience training schools require dogs to be at least 6 months old.
- *Practice, practice, practice:* take time on a daily basis to reinforce the behaviors you've taught your dog by practicing with him.

And I promise that I will be your loyal friend ... for all the days of my life.

CHAPTER 4
Love Journal

Who Am I?

My name is:

I was born on:

My mother's name is:

My father's name is:

I came from   kennel

I came from a litter of   sisters and   brothers:

I was adopted on:

What Do I Like?

Favorite Toys:

Favorite Walks:

Favorite Pals:

Favorite Humans:

Favorite Treats:

Favorite Things To Do:

Funniest Habits:

Who Takes Care Of Me

My Veterinarian:
_____
_____
_____

My Groomer:
_____
_____
_____

My Dog Sitter:
_____
_____
_____

My Trainer:
_____
_____
_____

Others:
_____
_____
_____

Memories

Memories

Memories

Memories